LETTER FROM THE EDITORS

Growth is inevitable. Even if one may not be aware of the changes one goes through, the evidence is clear once you take a moment to reflect. Which is why for this month we have decided to shed light on our METAMORPHOSIS. We focus on the places that have left a footprint and molded us into the person that we are today. We dive deep and analyze on the people that have come to our lives and changed us in one way or the other.

You are not the same person you were a year ago. We invite you to look in the mirror and really pay close attention to those changes that have been placed on your face and body. What do you see? Is there a glow radiating from you? Are your shoulders a bit slumped from all the weight you've been carrying? Do you see some lines gracing the corners of your lips from all the smiles that have welcomed your days?

In this issue, we open up about our METAMORPHOSIS and share with you what changed us for the better or for the worse, but ultimately has made us into the people we are today. We hope once your eyes take in the poetry, art and photos that confesses those changes, that you take the time to analyze what elements have made you begin your own METAMORPHOSIS.

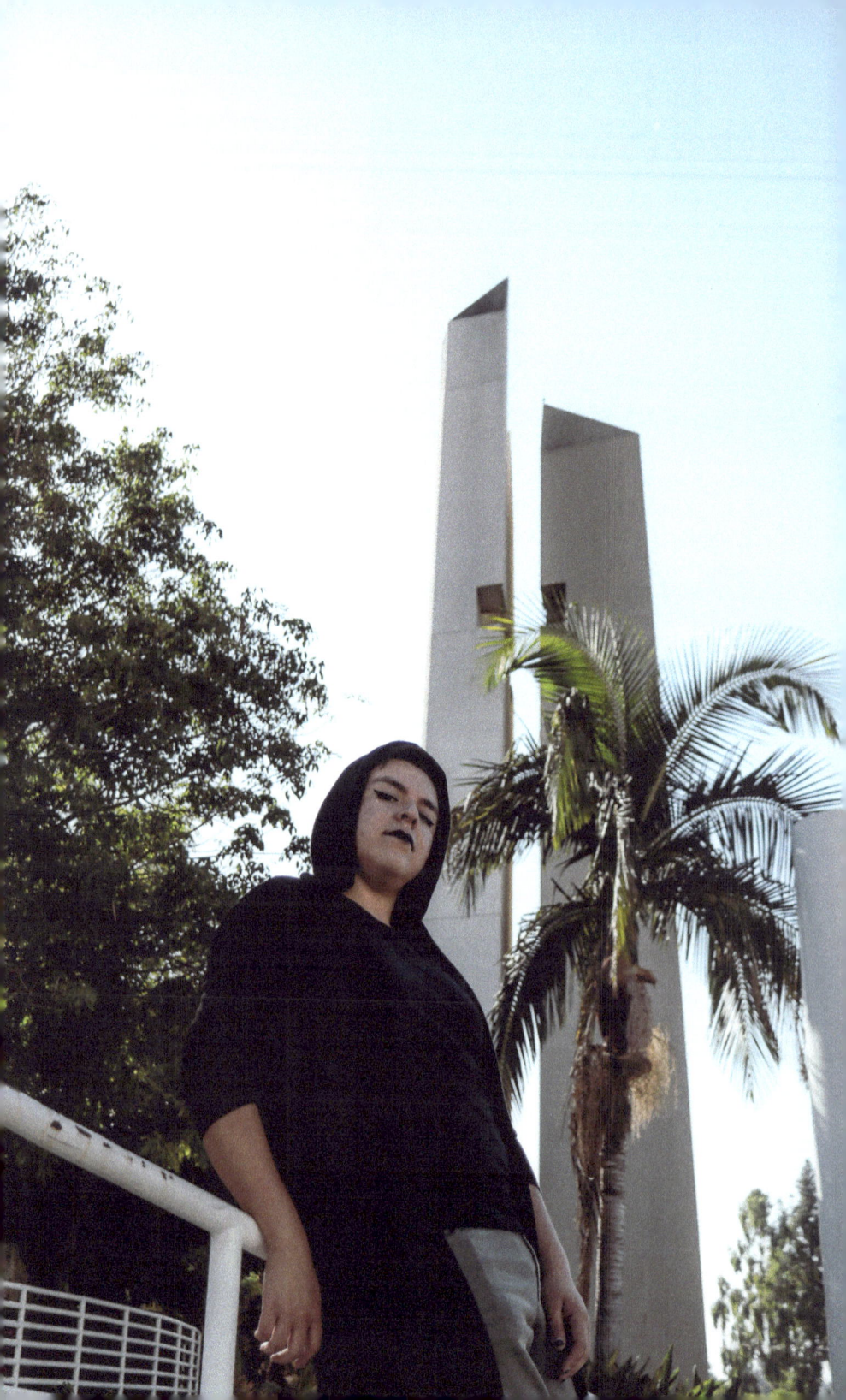

5	JOEY REYES IN ALL THEIR GLORY
8	THE TIME IN TWO YEARS
11	FINDING SELF
12	CHURCH AT THE TITANIC
14	LONELY GIRL IN MÉXICO
16	NEW ORLEANS
19	BIRTHDAY
21	I STOPPED DREAMING

EDITORIAL SHOOT
Photographer: Josephine Jael Jimenez
Model: Joey Reyes

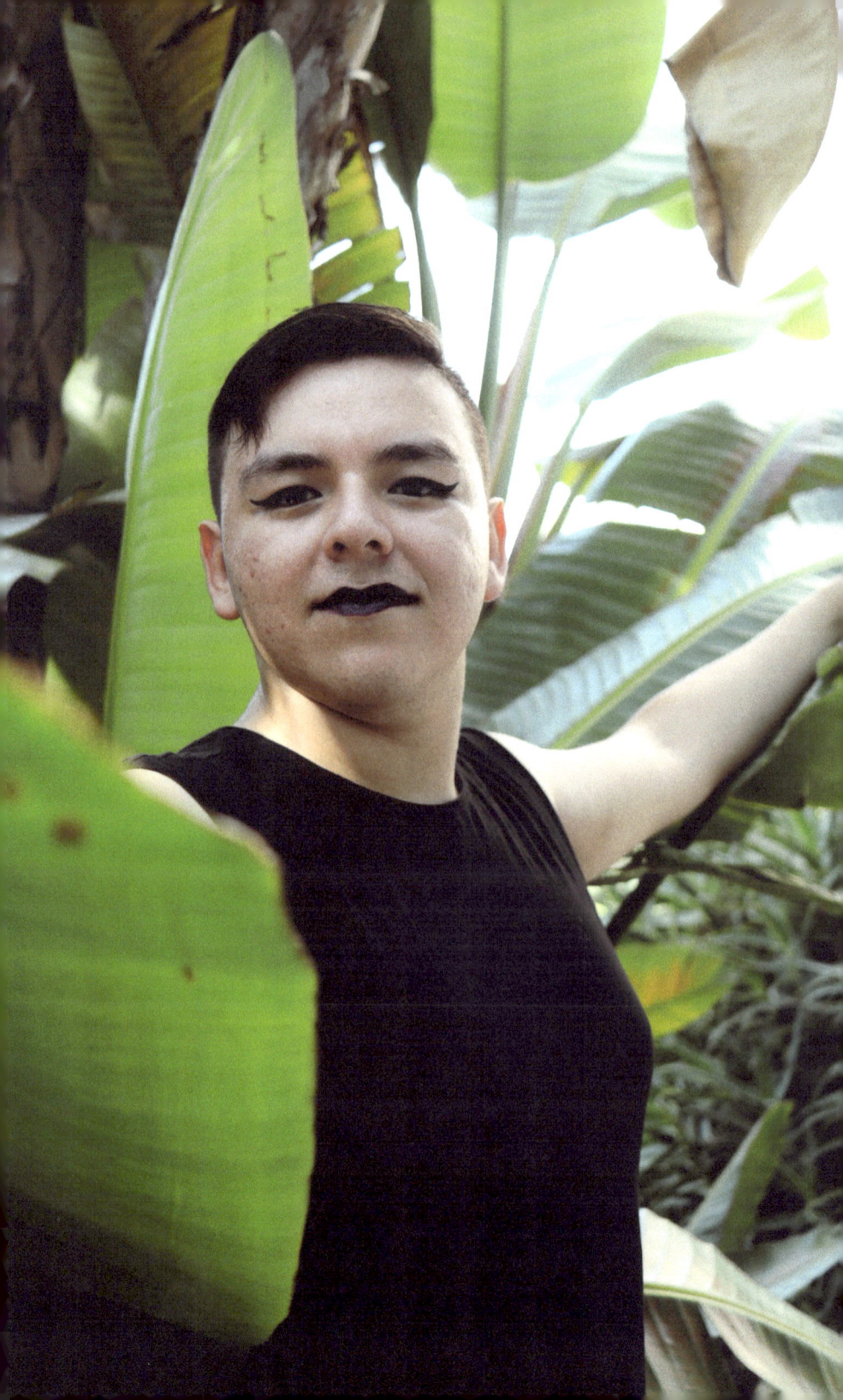

JOEY REYES
IN ALL THEIR GLORY

INTERVIEWED BY
JOSEPHINE JAEL JIMENEZ

What was the biggest life-altering event or moment that changed your life?

"It might sound like a cliche, but moving away from California in August 2017 was a pivotal moment in my life. I had moved to Cleveland to participate in an apprenticeship program at the Cleveland Playhouse and this was ultimately a bridge to the even bigger step of moving to New York City to pursue my career in the theater-making field. Up until this point, I had always lived in California and home was a hop, skip, and a jump away. This was now my time to truly be independent and cultivate my chosen family away from my given family.

The intention was to be in Cleveland for 10 months before making the shift to New York, but for various reasons, I ended up leaving the apprenticeship program 7 months early and I was caught at a crossroad of having to decide whether to go back to California and regroup or bite the bullet and hit the ground running in New York. With $200 in my bank account and my life packed into one suitcase and a duffel bag, I made the move to New York City on November 6th, 2017."

In what ways has this change most impacted your life?

"I don't think there is any way in which this change didn't impact my life. In the first month of living in New York, I stayed in 4 different apartments: staying with friends, friends of friends, and subletting through Thanksgiving. I very quickly had to learn how to be resourceful in a city I'd never even visited prior to moving to it. Those first 3 months really tested my patience and forced me to strategize how best to navigate a world that I had very little experience in. As someone who learned by the time they graduated from college that they wanted to grow into a future leader in their industry, I knew that I had my work cut out for me and as much as I thought I was ready, nothing could've prepared me for the unknown. I had moved to the biggest city for an industry that has continued to be predominantly operated by and curated for cisgendered, white people and it became a daily affirmation to myself that I belonged in these spaces and had the right to claim that space on behalf of myself and other marginalized communities. I began to cultivate and strengthen my voice, not only as an artist, but also as an advocate."

Would you say that you are better off than you used to be?

"I think that's very nuanced. In a lot of ways, yes, I am much better off than I used to be. I am fortunate enough to be in spaces and have a beautiful support system of people that have encouraged and nurtured me to continue to grow into a more realized version of myself. I have never been more in touch with my mind, body, and spirit and it's incredible to experience alongside others.

However, I'm a big believer that growth doesn't come without some pains. My mental health is something I've struggled with for at least 10 years and while I've learned how to manage it along the way, it has also grown difficult to manage at times. The pace of life in New York City waits for absolutely no one and, if you're not remaining aware, you can easily get swept up by the current. I've definitely had my moments where my mental state has grown totally exhausted and I've had to learn how to nurture that in a way that is different from when I lived and worked in California. It has ultimately taught me to really listen to my body and quiet my mind."

In what ways has this change affected your creative life?

"There has been greater intention in my work since experiencing this change. I believe part of that is voluntary and involuntary. Being forced to grow and move at a pace that you may not be used to is almost traumatizing, so I've had to carve out moments in my life to be able to reflect and meditate peacefully in order to understand who I am becoming and how I want my creative life to reflect that. I don't think I would've been brave enough to start to explore my writing voice on my own and that's why I'm forever grateful for Young Ignorantes. The intentionality behind the publication is what really convinced me that my work was worthy being printed and shared with others."

What is the biggest lessons you've learned since this metamorphosis occurred?

"Patience. Patience. Patience. Ironically, moving to what is most likely the fastest city in the world, my biggest lesson has been patience and it's a lesson that I continue to practice every single day. I cannot speak for others, but I believe it's a common feeling for those of us who come from marginalized backgrounds to have the feeling that you are never achieving enough, quickly enough. As someone who aspires to be a leader in my field, that feeling heightens even more. It's truly a discipline to extend grace and patience with yourself and understand that your journey moves at its own pace and not at the pace of any other. I think we have trouble accepting that reality a lot. When we, as marginalized people, enter spaces that were not created with us in mind, we tend to overcompensate and over exhaust ourselves at the expense of our personal truths and identities. Those costs are far too great to sacrifice. I value myself too much to sacrifice myself for cheap and unfulfilling gratitude. What's that saying? Something along the lines of, 'It's not about the destination. It's about the journey.'"

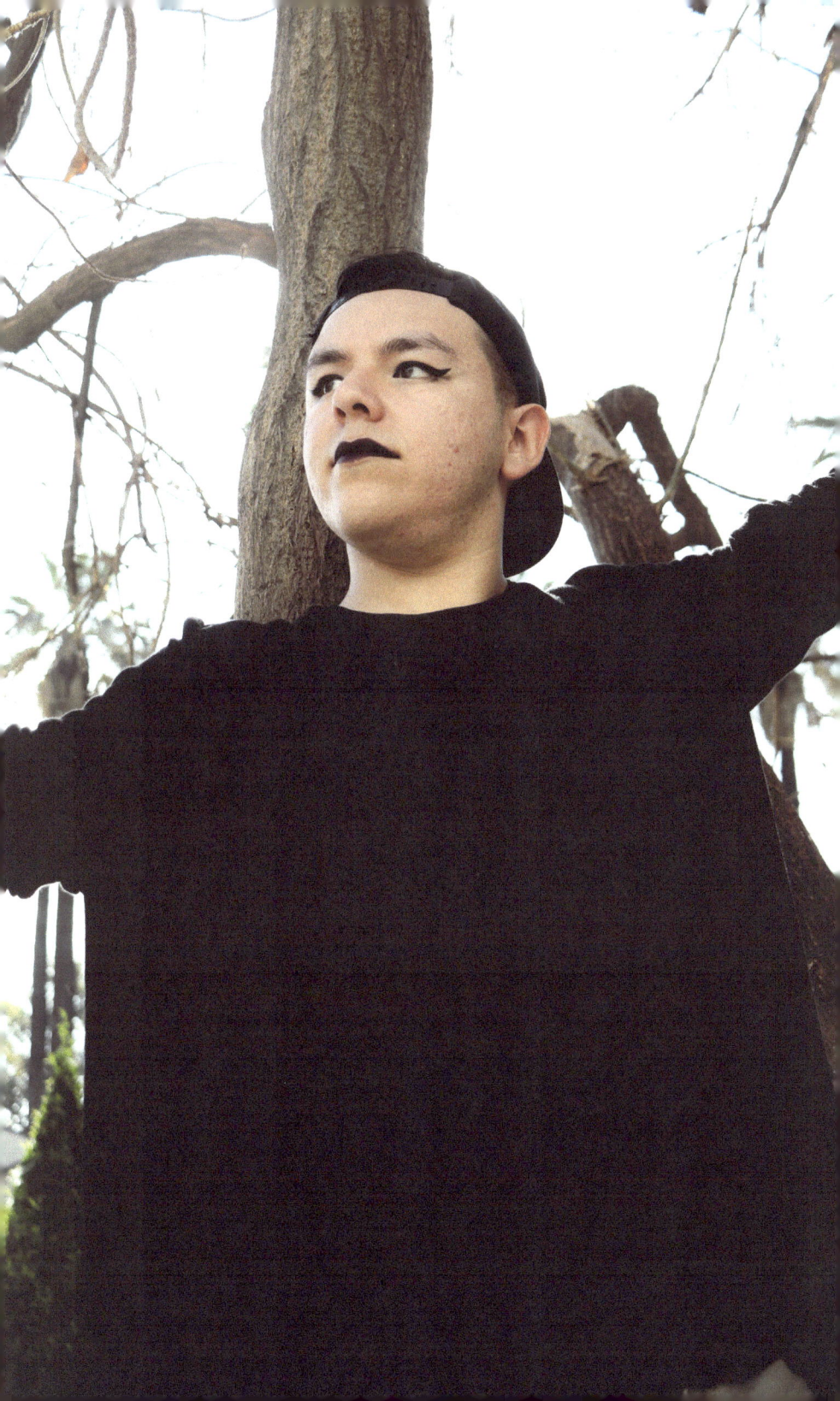

The Time in Two Years

CARLY BELL

A bit over two years ago I moved across an ocean into a land where people call sandwiches "sangas" and pronounce z as "zed." It wasn't supposed to be a long adventure, 6 or 8 months maximum, and I definitely wouldn't find love as all my aunts and friends surmised. I was wrong on both counts, but to be honest I'm not writing this to tell you about how moving across an ocean and falling in love "changes you" - because goodness haven't we all heard THAT story a million times.

No, instead I'm here to tell you that two years changes a person. To tell you that losing so many friends that you're terrified of making new ones, finding yourself involved in manipulative (and borderline abusive) relationships, starting a digital business while living in a country that systemically limits their access to high-speed internet and in many ways is a decade behind the U.S., fighting through and decimating urges to consistently self-sabotage, getting angrier than you ever have in your entire life (daily, for six months), moving and moving and moving again and again and again changes you.

You see I, like many of you, spend a lot of time on social media. I actually work on social media, but I'll refrain from my urge to say so I have it even worse than you (whoops, nevermind). As I'm sure you're aware: you see a lot of shit on social media. Not poo (thank god), but like - people who make $10,000 seemingly overnight and people who are just SO happy about the relationship they manifested and people who are traveling the world like OMG LIFE IS SO GOOD all the damn time. That sort of shit.

And when I saw that shit over the last two years, I was like: is no one else struggling? Am I alone in this? Followed by: wait, am I that person on social media too?

Two years of life experience included about one year of trying to convince everyone else (including myself) that I was fine, so much so that until about a week ago I entirely romanticized a super shitty neighborhood bar just because someone I once knew really liked it and apparently I had forgotten how to have an opinion. That year was then followed by a year where I became a shadow of myself and screamed one night at a person I love that this is me now why can't

"Hay más tiempo que vida..."

you just accept it! Stop asking me to be who I was, she's gone forever!

It was true in a way, that she was gone. But truth be told I'm re-becoming her, only this time she's stronger and sexier and healthier and happier than she ever could have been before, all because of all of the fucking awful experiences that life has given me over the last two years which, from the outside, appears to simply be me moving across an ocean and falling in love.

If you've watched my life on social media for the last two years, I can guarantee you haven't seen the half of it. If you have no idea who I am and are wondering why on earth I'd think that you've seen my life on social media, the same message can be translated to literally anyone else. This isn't a tirade against social media (I work on it, remember), but I guess a reminder that social media is a virtual reality that even the best of the best get sucked into believing is real and normal. And if you're feeling like you're riding the struggle bus alone because everyone else has their shit together - I can promise you that that isn't the case.

Oh, and I guess the whole purpose of this piece was to talk about the things that change us, to answer the question, what made you burst from your chrysalis? And, well, my answer to that is: time. Time and a whole lotta dedication to keep putting one foot in front of the other, even when it felt like I was waist-deep in cement.

A letter written to my favorite author reminded her that, "Hay más tiempo que vida," or, there is more time than life. As I think about the fact that time has changed me so thoroughly, has brought me out of the dark chrysalis that I lived in in some way or another for nearly my entire life, I consider the life that has happened in that time, and the life that will continue happening as I continue through my time of being alive. Though it would be right to say that the events of my life have been the catalyst for change, I'm standing firm on the fact that it is the time that I allowed myself to walk, rest, stop, go back, run, sprint, and pause that cemented, or finalized, the change. The last two years have been filled with a lot, but it's the liminal space, the moments in-between, the seconds or days of "nothing" that truly created "something." They created the woman I am today.

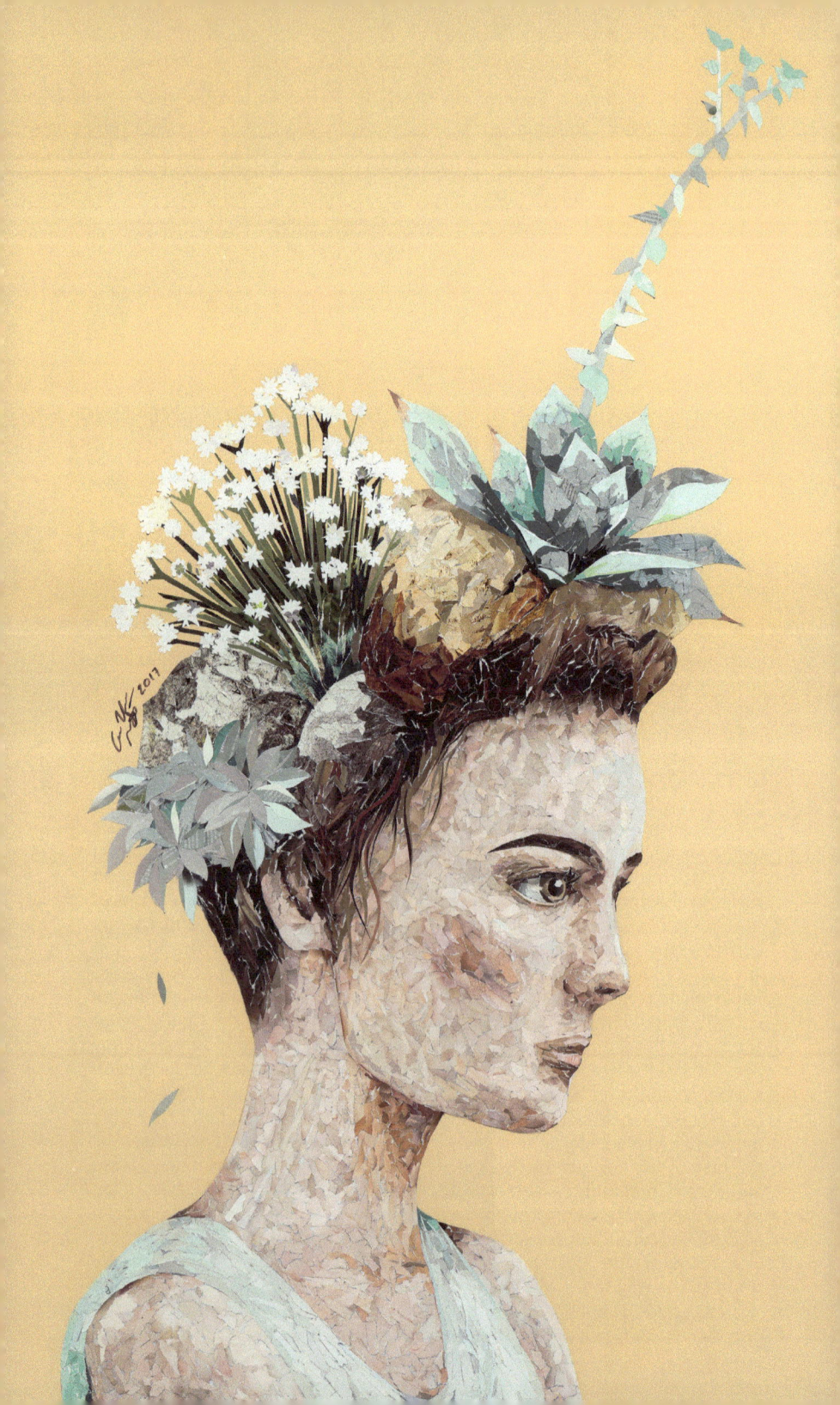

Finding Self

JOHN PEÑA

I find that life is an ongoing journey of finding oneself. Especially through all the labels and barriers that capitalism and colonialism puts on us. I, like anyone else reading this exist after several centuries of displacement, and abuse. Being of Diaspora can feel like a constant struggle for safety and understanding, living within systems that literally aren't built to nurture any of the healing we need.

So many of us feel lost because the language used to describe us, our bonds, and spirituality; were destroyed, our connections to each other and land severed. The forms of these teachings that survived are suppressed, mistreated, or appropriated for "cultural" Consumption to this day. Many generations ago we were placed into colonial boxes, where anything that wasn't gendered or white was just "Other". Other to varying degrees but still other nonetheless.

That "Other" was and still is beautiful and to find ourselves beautiful is a necessary act of revolution.

Every Conversation with a Diasporic sibling, is creating a new language that affirms our shared understanding or confusion at the systems that aim to keep us down. Our discourse currently wedged somewhere between ancestral knowledge and Millenial Socio cultural analysis with no direction in a world facing collapse.

Lots of us struggling to let go of the societal need for consumption and embracing a natural desire for spiritual growth and collective Liberation, while facing barriers, and crises created by western exceptionalism. We are at a powerful point in our humanity, where the deafening isolation that capitalism created is clashing with our desire for interdependence, and liberation.

I am transformed each day with the experiences and conversations I have with folks who like myself are trying to find the meaning of life in Diaspora, and how to destroy colonial structures, and the various chains that bind. Impatiently preparing, while trying to reconnect not only with each other; but ourselves. Before it's too late.

Dudleya
Collage *by Victoria Molina Vargas*

Church at the Titanic

ADAEZE NKWOCHA

I sat in the back of the car silent. It was as if they couldn't see me, or just didn't want to. We had been on the road for some time, on the way to a new church my parents wanted to try. I never really knew what difference it made what church we went to. It wasn't like we'd be any more saved than the last time. Every Sunday at 9:30 am I would acquire an acute case of restless leg syndrome. My knees knocked together and my toes tingled ready to dance out of the building as fast as I could as soon as the service was over. Church was a beauty pageant where the contestants' scores were based on how well they could make up their transgressions. A bunch of bullshit covered with sprinkles. Why we had to drive so far to be saved never resignated with me.

I was busy using my eyes to jump over street shadows as we drove down Main St.; a game that I used to hack away at the uncomfortable seconds of the car ride left. My brothers and sister were birds, chirping away at each other in the front seat. They were busy exchanging lines from a movie they had watched the other night at the theaters; an outing I wasn't invited to and was pretending as if I didn't want to be anyway. I was used to the cold shoulder by now. The silence that once cut like a dagger now only felt like a paper cut, stinging only if I touched it and I never dared to.

We rounded the corner. My dad was in the driver's seat, humming away to the song playing on the radio while tapping his fingers on the steering wheel. I wanted him to give me one of those reassuring looks in the rearview mirror, the one that let me know everything was going to be okay. But he stared straight ahead, never diverting his eyes from the road except for to chime in with my siblings and their conversation every once in a while. A part of me wanted to chime in too but was scared of the rejection. I couldn't even remember how long it had been since I had last spoken to them. It had to have been months by now. How cruel it was to be inches from my family but still feel so far away; how cruel it was to be forced so far away. I missed them but it seemed as if they didn't think twice about me. So it was easier to stay forgotten, to blend in with the street shadows I was constantly jumping over. Tears welled in my eyes, and I prayed to God I wouldn't cry. Not now. Who knew one picture could cause such a big rift. Who knew liking a boy could wreak all this havoc. I no longer fit into their box, even if it was made out of sand. I pressed my back against the seat wanting to sink deeper and deeper until I disappeared. "Hello? Does anybody notice me?" I wanted to scream. Did I notice me? This time their cold shoulder hit like an iceberg, and I the Titanic. I felt myself floating in the water; was I Jack or was I Rose? At this point, it didn't matter. I was dead in the water and alone on my raft; floating aimlessly through what I thought was supposed to be family.

Church was in sight now. Time slowed down as we got closer to the fraudulent asylum. My family gathered themselves, their faces painted with smiles as if the devil didn't know their sins. They took their places among the contestants. Their comedy act performance taking the win. I knew this church would not be it. My mom would tell us all to pay close attention to the sermon, like she always does, while all the while thinking of an

> **"The silence that once cut like a dagger now only felt like a paper cut, stinging only if I touched it and I never dared to."**

excuse for us to not come back. She'd complain and say she didn't like the music or that the pastor didn't speak to her enough. I wondered if that was really it or if she just wasn't listening. She had a habit of that.

I've never felt God in any church, always in the silence of my room. I found him there one night sitting on the edge of my bed, waiting for me to wake up from the nightmare he knew I was having. We'd stay up all night gossiping like little girls about what I had dreamed of. Even though he already knew what was in my heart he let me speak anyways. Then he told me, in the midst of the silence, that it was okay not to smile, and that His castles aren't made out of sand. At that very moment his words hit like an iceberg, and I the Titanic. At this point it didn't matter, I was Jack and I was Rose. I had let go, and I had survived. Though, freezing and cold, still I rose.

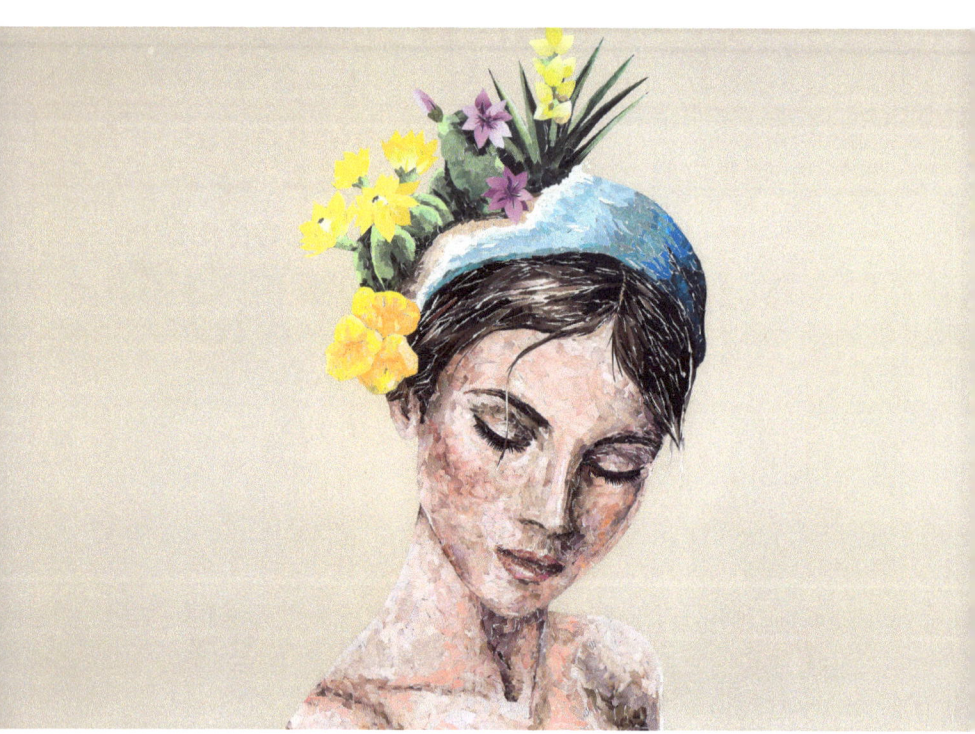

Lonely Girl in México

BRENDA HERNÁNDEZ JAIMES

Mazatlanensis
Collage by Victoria Molina Vargas

It was in mi bello México where I became the woman that I am today.

Living without seeing my parents every day, quickly help me shed any childhood behavior I had held onto.

The first few months in México I was preparing for mis quince, the party that would introduce me as an adult woman.

After that night I battled with depression and tried not to drown it by focusing on the goals that had fueled me to move to México.

I would force myself not to cry and tell mi mamá, 'te extraño'.

My aunt would say that if I did that I would only make mi mamá feel bad for letting me live in México.

Mi mamá had enough to worry about and I didn't want to overwhelm her with my "teenage hormones".

Not many people know this, but the first three years were bleak.

By day I would bury myself in school and improving mi Español, so I could pass my subjects

By night I would feel so lonely and distract myself with watching movies and reading.

But I had nights where I would cry into my pillow and imagine the life I would build for myself once I graduated from high school and university.

Looking back, I would just hug that lonely girl and tell her that everything would be okay.

That it was okay to tell mi mamá that she missed her, she was missing her too.

That life wouldn't end up as she had imagined as, it actually turned out even better.

Less lonely and more fulfilled.

I would tell her to keep her chin up, that her passion and drive would help her mold the woman she would become.

The woman that I am now.

The first three years in México weren't all sunshine, but the eight years in México were beautiful.

I lived my childhood dream of living in my ancestors country, improve mi Español, and lived the wonderful and terrible experiences that shaped me.
And I wouldn't have it any other way.

NEW ORLEANS

REBEKAH HOOGERWERF

5/15/19

I've been in New Orleans since Sunday for a convention for work and overall it's been an interesting experience. Going out on my own while out of town feels very different from when I do it at home. A lot of people have acted very surprised to find out I'm doing this all by myself and it reminds me how glad I am to be this independent and confident in myself. I have tomorrow and Friday all to myself and that really is an intimidating experience. I'm so proud of myself for going through this on my own. I feel more motivated to work harder and get things changed in the [trampoline] park. On a separate note, I'm doing my best to stop thinking about Will. I do still miss Will and when I drink especially, I consider how bad would it really be to let him know that? I know I deserve better. I deserve someone that would miss me and tell me that. I deserve someone that will value my independence and view me the way I view myself. Clearly that's not Will and I have to let go of the positive memories I have of him so that I can better embrace the potential with anyone else. I know what I'm worth and one day I'll find someone that will recognize that worth and it'll be well worth the wait and pain I've gone through.

5/16/19

Last night was one of the coolest and weirdest and most unexpected nights of my life. At the end of the convention, we had a police escort as we followed a band in parade-like fashion down Bourbon Street to a bar that was rented out for an awards ceremony and after party. We threw beads off a balcony at people walking down the street and it was one of the most perfect moments of my life. I got along well with a bunch of the guys from corporate and that made me feel good about myself. The entire night I was talking to this guy named David. We met at Mardi Gras World the first night and I immediately thought he was cute. He's a manager for a [trampoline] park in Connecticut and we had some good conversations prior to last night as well. Last night we finally actually had time to really talk about non work-related things and it was so fun. Eventually, we left the party together to walk back to the hotel. I made the move and held his hand as we walked. When we got back, we stood in the elevator and kissed for the first time. We got back to my room and kissed some more, but he had a flight early in the morning and couldn't stay long. He told me I'm beautiful and this entire convention he liked me but was intimidated. He told me to never stop being who I am. He said it sucks we live so far away, but we'll see each other again some day. He said he believes we were supposed to meet each other. He thinks I'm amazing and chill and that I deserve to be treated better. I can't believe last night happened.

5/17/19

My flight back to LA is tonight and I'm so sad this trip is over. I'm sad about David. Thinking back on everything he said, I'm not really sure he plans on talking to me. It just sucks because I want to get to know him more. But he made it clear that the more we talk, the harder it would be. There was something special about him. Like as soon as we met, I felt this connection to him that I just can't comprehend. This week was a much needed break from my everyday life and I wish I could relive it. There isn't a thing I regret. It was perfect. Even if I never hear from David again, I'm glad it happened because it made me feel confident and special and it reminded me that there are plenty of guys out there that are interested in me.

5/18/19

After thinking about it some more, I realized David is just as much of an asshole as all other guys. He liked me for the week, but had no desire to continue communicating with me. And he was just nice to me because he wanted to have sex with me. I texted him today and he basically said he'll see me at the next corporate event, so I take that as I'll never see him again. The hopeless romantic in me really wanted to stay in touch with him. I just hate that these seemingly romantic stories keep happening to me only to turn into nothing. I'm still holding on to the hope that I'll hear from Will again. I think about him often. I don't think I'll get over him until there's someone else in my life. I was so happy in New Orleans. So far today, I already feel that trapped feeling being back here. Like I already need to go on another vacation. Is this just how life is for everyone? Is everyone bored of the mundane and only happy when routines are broken? We're really all unhappy. I don't know what it will possibly take for me to be satisfied with my everyday life. As much as I feel depressed and unhappy with my life, deep down there's another side of me that is truly content. I know that seems to contradict itself, but maybe that's the gray area my therapist is always talking about. Part of my depression just stems from not knowing how long this "content" feeling will last. I want to continue to grow so I need to continue to make changes in my life, but I don't know what changes will make me content. And is content even what I'm striving for, or is there more to life than just being content? The reason I'm so indecisive is because I just freeze whenever I start thinking about these things. I guess life isn't just miserable until you finally "achieve" happiness. It's a constant going back and forth. Everything's gray. I'm both happy and depressed at the same time because life is full of gray areas. Not everything is black and white.

5/22/19

My trip to New Orleans made me realize how confident I can be. The whole trip I was completely myself, but I was doing things I don't normally do. I confidently introduced myself to strangers and communicated body language that showed how confident I am in myself. My therapist pointed out that maybe David wasn't just trying to get in my pants. Sure, I may have disappointed him by not having sex with him, but that's not necessarily the only reason why he doesn't want to talk to me. He's had his own shit happen in his life to make him not want to do something long distance and that's valid. I have worked so fucking hard to create this life for myself. I could've taken the easy way out and moved back home when things got hard, but I didn't. I have stuck through the hard countless times and I am so proud of myself. I have worked my ass off at my job, in therapy, and in my relationships to get myself to where I am today. I have no idea what's in store for me the rest of this year. I couldn't even begin to predict what my life will look like on December 31st. It's ok to be where I'm at right now. I'm happy. A little bit bored, but happy. I'm excited to see how different things will be at the end of this year and how unexpected the changes in my life will be. Life is full of surprises and I have a feeling this year is going to bring some pretty big surprises. The first half of this year has emotionally been so shitty, but I refuse to allow the rest of this year to feel that way that often. I'm determined to do what I do best and work through the hard to become stronger and make my life better.

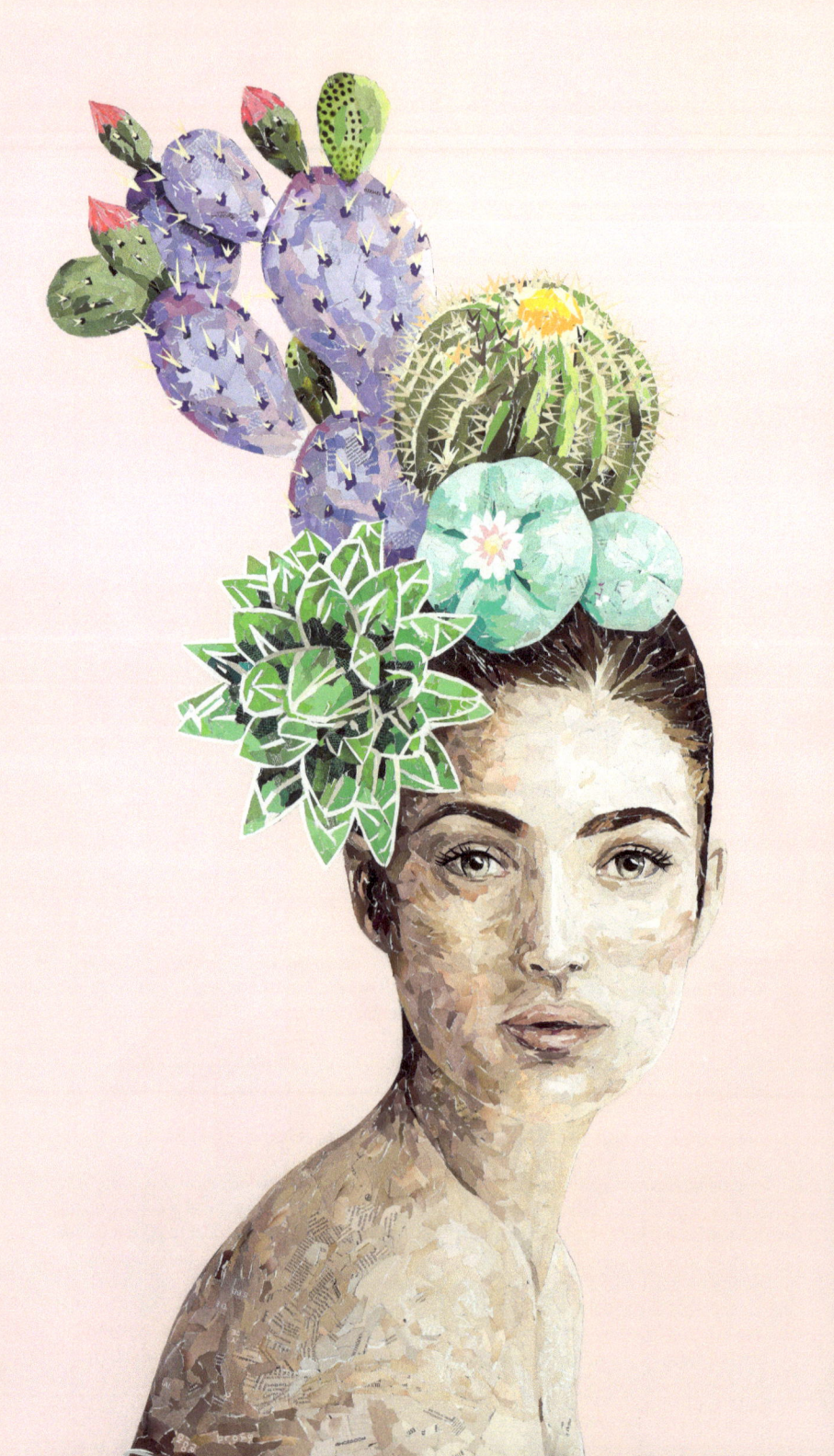

Birthday

MELISSA ARELLANO

Happy birthday to me,
I softly sing.

Wishes flowing in the breeze,
as I look back
at who I used to be.
I've strayed so far from who I was
that I don't recognize
this reflection standing before me.
Scars that lie just beneath the surface
waiting to softly pull me under,
reminding me of the dreams I had
that weren't strong enough to fly, so they drowned.

Happy birthday to me.

Another year, another year older.
I'm not where I expected to be at this age
so naturally I'm reluctant to turn this new page.
I'm afraid of starting a whole new chapter,
but hopefully this will be the one where I grow wings.

Agave Reina Victoria
Collage *by Victoria Molina Vargas*

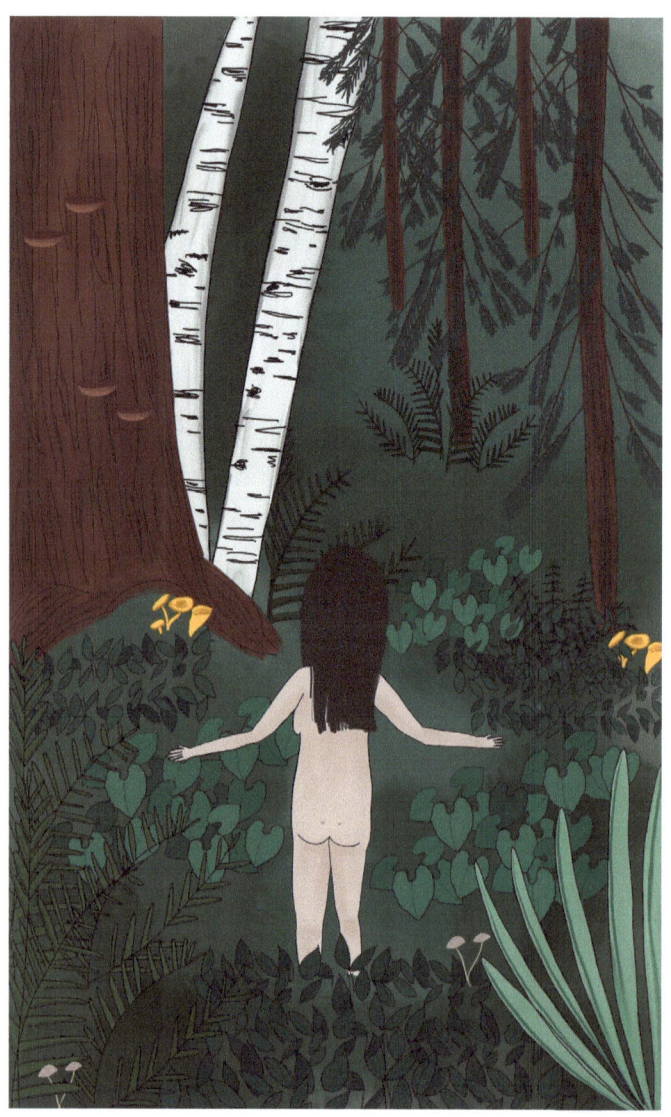

Illusatration by Melissa Lee

THE VICE COLUMN

I Stopped Dreaming

Josephine Jael Jimenez

I stopped dreaming today and yesterday and for a while now. Most days, I convince myself to let my dreams go into the wind and find someone who wants to hold them and love them and keep them, but they never leave in their fullness. Scraps of each always remain and grow no matter how much I refuse to water them. My breath is their sunlight. I've started to realize that some part of them will probably stay with me as long as I live, but I've decided to stop letting them creep into my heart and soul. I have to accept these dreams are not mine to hold anymore.

Because they will not leave me, I have decided to try to change them. It's a long process full of patience that I have never been blessed with and care that I have never really had use for. Everyday I graft a little piece of a new life on to these dreams and hope they'll take. Sometimes they don't and sometimes they do, but still I clip and cut and tear at these dreams that keep growing back in the hope that they'll evolve with me.

Way back when, I used to strive to be President of the United States of America. My little hands thought they could mold a better world, but as I grew and grew and learned and learned, I realized that I have no interest in being the President of the United States of America or the United States of America at all. That dream died without a fight when it saw the world for what it was.

Then I thought I could be a woman in a suit in a tall building surrounded by men in suits. Hell hath no fury like a woman under a glass ceiling, but hell is more patient than a free spirit in an accounting class. Readily and easily, I leapt from the tall building and into the arms of writing and art, thinking I would pursue the notoriety that I suppose we all crave. This is the dream that holds fast, an abstract vision full of books and shows and people I've never met. It's a dream I found in college and that stopped fitting quite right after life slowed down from being a full time student and a full time broken heart just trying to survive. As much as I am the same wild, chaotic woman as I was in college, I've also evolved into a version of myself that is slightly less wild and chaotic. It's not much of a chance, but it's enough to make my dreams feel heavy.

Success looks different to me now. It's hazier than it used to be. The view is less cluttered with buildings and traffic and more full of trees and trails leading far into some forest I've never been to. For whatever reason, there is nothing I crave more now than peace. No corporate ladder is tall enough to reach for the peace in my mind that I crave so desperately. There is no mountain of money big enough to make me feel like I could be stable because I'm far too familiar with stories of that climb. I remember people talking about peace being the

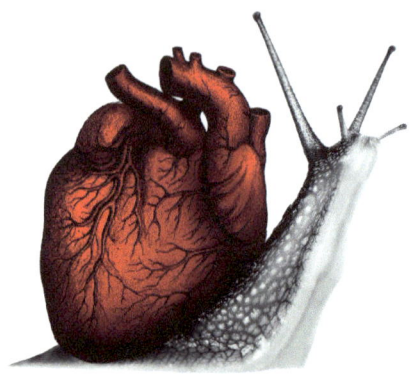

only thing we should pursue and now I finally understand what that means.

Maybe it's the love I found that makes me feel this way. For the first time in a long time, I don't feel the need to find the escape route out of the life I have. This doesn't feel temporary because in my heart of hearts and in the most logical parts of my mind, I know it's not temporary. I have found a love the good Lord intended for me to feel worthy of and nothing feels better than to feel like home. Never never never did I think I would feel elated at the thought of heading home everyday or homesick when I'm away, but here I am perpetually homesick when I'm not in the solace of my peace.

Dreams of American success and making a million dollars seem like dreams that would take me away from this state of life I find myself in, so instead I'm trying to wrap my mind around a type of success that I make for myself.

I make art for myself now, to free my mind and rid myself of burdens I no longer wish to carry. I write for the sake of writing now, without deadlines or any sense of urgency. All my creative pursuits have evolved into pursuing creativity with my community instead of chasing after numbers. It's all so slow and so much more pure and it's hard to believe I ever wanted anything else. Even when I can't perfectly stay on this new path I'm on, I try to remember to come back. There are times when I still feel like I want traditional success and money to burn, but then I hear the voices of thousands of parents and more adultier adults passing down ancient wisdom I'd be stupid for not remembering: Needs come before wants. I don't need the success that white men told me I should strive for and practically die for. I need peace.

Because even in my hustle and bustle of my old dream days, I subconsciously sought out a slower pace of life. Trip after trip was spent doing nothing with good people who loved me. From the streets of Ireland to an Army base in Alabama, the only places I ever ran to in my time away from working towards these dreams I can't dream anymore were places where people waited to count the slower hours with me. Long walks and talks were what I missed when I came back home and it's only now that I realize that my body and my heart and my soul were crying out for me to find this type of peace everyday instead of making it a drug I only indulge in on vacation. I'm finally listening because I am finally trying to accept that my life is not long enough to continue with these pursuits that every cell in my body is rejecting.

Maybe I'll start dreaming again when my dreams finally evolve into what I need them to be, but right now it just feels good to slow down, no matter how bad I am at staying in that pace.

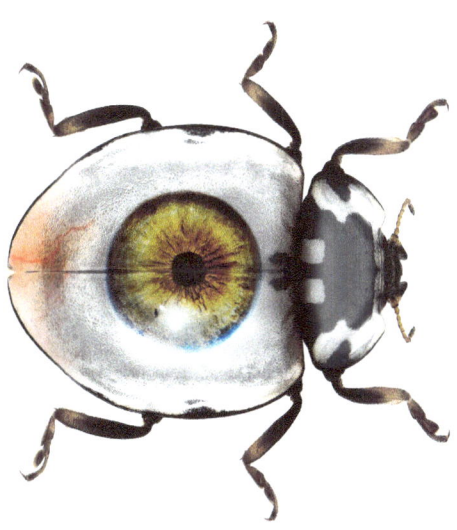

Corazón de Caracol (Left) & Eye Beatle (Above)
Art by Ricardo Cortés

Adaeza Nkwocha, @dayy.dayy1, aknkwocha.com, centrlave.wordpress.com
Brenda Hernández Jaimes, Editor and Head Writer, @bren_jai
Carly Bell, @itsmecjb
Joey Reyes, @joeykangarooooo
John Peña, Founder of @ReinaProjectNY
Josephine Jael Jimenez, Editor & Designer-in-Chief, @josietakestheworld
Melissa Arellano, @melspetals
Melissa Lee, @thehouseoflees
Rebekah Hoogerwerf, twitter: @bhoog
Ricardo Cortés, @rcortesc
Victoria Molina Vargas, @artvictoriam, victoriamolina.mx
Young Ignorantes, @youngignorantes, youngignorantes.com